Boys Can Be Angels Too

Abingdon Press

Nashville

Boys Can Be Angels Too

Copyright © 2003 by Abingdon Press

0-687-06517-8

03 04 05 06 07 08 09 10 11 12 - 10 9 8 7 6 5 4 3 2 1

Manufactured in the United States of America

Contents

Can We Have a Real Tree for Christmas?

A STORY OF CHANGING TIMES AND ENDURING TRUTHS

By Sue Rood

Production Notes

While the tree is being decorated on the left side of the stage, the creche will take form on the right side of the stage. The stable can be placed on the stage before the play. It can be as simple as a frame that suggests a stable. An electric star should be placed on the stable. Straw can be placed in the center surrounding the crib where Jesus will lay. A bail of straw can be placed behind the crib for Mary and Joseph to sit on.

Characters

Speaking roles:	Nonspeaking roles:
Narrator	Angels (younger children)
Reader 1	Mary
Reader 2	Joseph
Reader 3	Three wise men
Reader 4	Children to decorate tree
Reader 5	Children to stand by tree

Props

Evergreen tree, tree stand, stable, electric star, loose straw, bail of straw, crib, Christmas tree lights, Christmas tree tinsel, Christmas tree skirt (solid white), cut-out snowflakes, candy canes, angel tree topper, gold, frankincense, myrrh, gift-wrapped boxes, signs with months of the year on them (optional: costumes from other countries)

Scene One: Sixth graders

NARRATOR: The powerful, the common, the rich, the poor, the clergy, and the lay people have searched for centuries to discover what was so awesome about Jesus that caused people, years after his death, to write birth stories that appear only in Matthew and Luke. Jesus, the spirit person, so shone with the light of God's love that people were changed forever. They experienced Jesus like no other they had met. They, as we, tried to understand the mystery of Jesus. Then in the birth stories they set about to honor that mystery with miraculous stories. The two Christmas stories from Matthew and Luke that we are about to hear were written years after Jesus' birth. They were written in such a way as to honor the nature of Jesus. The story brings us hope that if God can be fully present in the person of Jesus who had human traits as we have, then God can live in us. By using Jesus as a model for our lives, we can shine God's light in the darkest places.

Someone reads John 8:12. Several class members bring in the Christmas tree and begin to set it up.

READER 1: Here is the tree for the Christmas program. Isn't it beautiful? It smells so good. The evergreen is very special. It stays green all through the year, even in the winter. Totally awesome.

READER 2: This can remind us that Christ's life was so extraordinary that not even death could separate him from us. His spirit of truth and love is with us right now and will be in this world forever.

READER 3: Let's put on some lights and see how that looks.

Audience and children sing the first verse of "O Christmas Tree" while the lights are being strung.

READER 4: We do good work. These lights didn't even get tangled. The tree is really coming to life.

READER 5: The sparkle of the lights reminds us that Christ is the light of the world. His light is the light that shows us the way when we are lost. When we feel afraid or alone, we can talk to God, and God will show us the way. The light of God shown through him so clearly that we came to know who God is just by learning about Jesus.

READER 1: Here is the tinsel. Let's put it on next.

READER 2:   Wow! Look how it reflects the lights and makes the tree sparkle.

READER 3:   Didn't Jesus say that we should shine God's light in the world? We are just like this tinsel. We can make the world sparkle with God's love.

Light the star on the stable, which is located on the stage opposite the tree.

NARRATOR *invites the audience to sing three verses of "Jesus Loves Me." Someone might show the audience how to say the chorus in sign language.*

<u>Scene Two</u>: Fifth graders

NARRATOR: Jesus broke down barriers of hate and discrimination. He lived a life that broke the cycle of violence in this world. Jesus saw the spirit of God in all people. He called them and calls us to love our neighbor, ourselves, and our enemies.

Someone reads Galatians 3:28.

READER 1:   Don't you think the tree needs a skirt?

READER 2:   A skirt? I didn't know trees wore skirts.

READER 3:   You know, this kind of skirt. (*Shows an all-white skirt for around the base of the tree*)

READER 4:   Oh, I see. It looks like snow around the tree. I sure hope we have snow for Christmas.

READER 1:   Have you ever looked at a snowflake? Those beautifully shaped crystals are all different. None of them are alike.

READER 5:   You are right. That little snowflake has a great message for us. God created us all differently as well—different sizes, shapes, colors, and talents. But we are all important in God's world. Jesus told us that we are all loved by God just the way we are.

READER 2:   I think maybe the snowflake tells us something else.

7

READER 1: What's that?

READER 2: Those little snowflakes add up to be a drift that can stop a whole city. If each of us began to see God in all we met, we could stop violence in our world.

They all put cut-out snowflakes on the backdrop behind the tree or hang them on the tree. Snowflakes can be cut from coffee filters. Put the skirt on the tree while the audience sings, "It's a Small World." Fifth graders dressed in hats or carrying props or wearing costumes from other countries stand to the side of the manger. Or invite members of your church from other countries to stand by the manger. They stay there during the other scenes while the others come to the manger.

NARRATOR *invites children and congregation to sing the first and third verses of "O Come All Ye Faithful."*

Scene Three: Fourth graders

NARRATOR: At the time of Jesus' birth, shepherds were seen on the hillsides watching their flocks. They were ordinary folk with little power. In Luke's story, they are the first to hear of Jesus' birth. The hope of love being born anew in the world was first shared with the shepherds. They in turn went out and told others of the new hope for the world born of a young woman in a lowly stable.

Someone reads Luke 2:8.

READER 1: What would Christmas be without candy canes? Yummy.

READER 2: Candy canes! What do they have to do with the Christmas story?

READER 1: Look at them. Do they remind you of anything?

READER 3: A sled runner!

8

READER 1: Well, that could be, but what would that have to do with the Christmas story? That belongs in the song, "Grandma Got Run Over by a Reindeer."

READER 4: A "J"?

READER 1: I guess the "J" could remind us of Jesus. But I was thinking about the shepherd's crook. Shepherds are an important part of the Christmas story. The tale in Luke tells us that Jesus' birth was first made known to the shepherds. This is amazing because shepherds were considered common workers in their time.

READER 2: Since the tale of Jesus' birth was written many years after he died, maybe they were trying to tell us that Jesus was a friend of all—the poor and the outcast.

READER 1: That would fit. Jesus always turned everything upside down.

READER 3: Yeah, like the tables of the money changers.

The children put the candy canes on the tree while they and the audience sing the first, fourth, and sixth verses of "While Shepherds Watch Their Flock by Night." Kindergartners and first-grade students gather around the nativity. They stay there for the remainder of the program.

Scene Four: Third graders

Someone reads Luke 2:8-14.

NARRATOR: In a story written to explain the awesomeness and pow-erfulness of God in Jesus' life, it would not do to have word of his birth spread by word of mouth. There would have to be a special messenger to deliver the word of God so profoundly known in the life of this man.

READER 1: What would a Christmas tree be without an angel on the top?

READER 2: Yes, of course, the angels are very important to our story. The angel gave a special meaning to the message that was given to the shepherds.

READER 3: What do you mean, "angel"? There was a multitude of angels.

READER 4: That's right. Our Sunday school teacher said a multitude. I think that means lots and lots.

READER 5: The angels told the shepherds where they could find the child lying in a manger. They went and found the baby. Then they went to tell others.

READER 1: Even then God needed messengers to tell people about Christ. God depends on all of us to be messengers of Christ's love in the world, to all and for all.

NARRATOR *directs audience in singing the first and second verses of* "Angels We Have Heard on High," *while the preschool angels come forward. They stay by the manger.*

A third-grade MARY *and* JOSEPH *enter with the baby and sit at the nativity, while the congregation sings the first verse of "Away in a Manger."*

Scene Five

Someone reads Matthew 2:1-12.

NARRATOR: We do know for sure that Jesus was born to a woman. Most likely she was very young and had shortcomings, as we all do. She was poor and powerless. She died a death, as we all do. She loved Jesus and cared for him as he was growing up. The son she nurtured was so spirit-filled that the presence of a star and wise men are used to honor him in the Book of Matthew.

READER 1: Now that we are through decorating the tree, there seems to be something missing.

READER 2: Yeah, we don't have any presents under the tree.

10

READER 3: The story of Jesus' birth in Matthew tells us that wise men who studied the sky, followed a special star that led them to Jesus. They brought Jesus gifts of gold, frankincense, and myrrh. Why would the story be told this way?

READER 5: Maybe because gold represents Jesus as king. Frankincense was used in worship, so it represented Jesus as a spirit person. Myrrh represented Jesus' death.

READER 1: Wow! Those are very special gifts to give. They must have been gifts of love.

Second-grade children bring gifts and place them under the tree. The three WISE MEN *come to the creche and bring their gifts of gold, frankincense, and myrrh. These could be junior-high youth.*

NARRATOR: Jesus came into history to give us the greatest gift of all—a glimpse of the power of love that lives in all of us. The life of Jesus gives us hope that if the spirit of God can live in all of us, along with all our human characteristics, then we have much more potential than we ever imagined. It gives us hope that God lives in each and every one of us. We need not be rich, educated, gifted, successful, wealthy, or powerful. God is within each of us. We can have a "real" tree for Christmas, whether the tree is fresh from the outdoors or artificial. If we put our symbols of love in Christ on the tree, our tree is real. It symbolized the "real" love of God shown to us in Christ.

As the audience sings "Away in a Manger," have people come up in order of their birthday month and place an offering in the manger for a preselected cause. Habitat for Humanity is excellent, since Mary and Joseph were homeless when Jesus was born. Have the NARRATOR *hold up signs with the months on them.*

Joy in the Manger

By Shirley Lockhart Ingram

Production Notes

Songs or carols can be sung by a choir, a children's choir, or the congregation.

Characters

Speaking roles:
Narrator
Angel
Readers

Nonspeaking roles:
Shepherds
Mary
Joseph
Three wise men

Props

Greenery, yule log, small Christmas tree, large Christmas card, poinsettia, large Christmas stocking, holly, large bell, jingle bells, candles for windows, wooden sheep, manger, gifts from wise men, Advent wreath

NARRATOR: Traditions are an important part of our heritage, especially at Christmas time. Some families gather on Christmas Eve or Christmas Day or another convenient day for all to eat together, exchange gifts, and renew family friendships. The children may play with their new toys and run and play with their cousins. Some families drive many miles. Some fly into crowded airports, and some may take the train. Why? The answer is simple: to be reunited with the people who raised us, people we grew up with, and a chance to spend time with people we love during this special season of love. Jesus' birth was an event for all to be one family—God's children.

NARRATOR: Now in medieval England, Christmas celebrations were mainly large feasts and festivities. For twelve days in the thirteenth century, Henry III butchered six hundred oxen for his Christmas feast. Quite a banquet!

Sing "The Twelve Days of Christmas." If you like, have twelve solos.

NARRATOR: Wassailing consisted of a house-to-house caroling party. The wassailers or carolers went around town on Christmas Eve, singing, and people invited them into their homes for something to eat and drink. The wassailers would bring holly or mistletoe to give to them. Then they were invited to come in and drink from the wassail bowl, which was a punch with spices, sugar, and apples. Christmas caroling originated from wassailing.

As the NARRATOR speaks, children go up and down the aisles handing out greenery to persons on the ends of the pews. Sing "Here We Come a Wassailing."

NARRATOR: The yule log was once a popular tradition. It was lit from a piece of last year's log and was supposed to burn to ashes all of last year's habits and experiences. A person could write down all of his or her grudges and bad thoughts on a piece of paper and throw them into the yule fire.

As the NARRATOR speaks, a child comes down the middle carrying a yule log. The child places it on the chancel rail and takes a seat behind the chancel rail. Sing "The First Noel."

NARRATOR: Martin Luther is credited with having the idea for the first decorated Christmas tree. Walking home one night, he looked up and saw the stars shining through the branches of an evergreen tree. Then he brought a tree into his home and fastened candles to its branches. Later the trees were decorated with popcorn, cranberries, tin stars, and colored paper rings. This custom came from Germany.

As the NARRATOR speaks, a child brings in a small Christmas tree. The child places it on the chancel rail and then takes a seat behind the chancel rail. Sing "O Christmas Tree" (or "Tannenbaum").

NARRATOR: Another custom from England is sending Christmas cards. The first Christmas card was believed to have been sent in England in 1846. Today Christmas cards are exchanged from mailbox to mailbox all over the world.

As the NARRATOR *speaks, a child brings in a large Christmas card. The child places it on the chancel rail and takes a seat behind the chancel rail.*

NARRATOR: A custom from Mexico is the beautiful poinsettia plant. In Mexico Christmas is celebrated from December 6 to January 6. Its leaves are shaped like a flaming red or white star to remind us of the star of Bethlehem. The center of the plant is shaped like a crown, like the ones the wise men wore.

As the NARRATOR *speaks, a child brings in a poinsettia. The child places it on the chancel rail and takes a seat behind the chancel rail. Sing "Feliz Navidad."*

NARRATOR: Children, do you know what *Feliz Navidad* means?

CHILDREN: (*In unison*) Merry Christmas!

NARRATOR: How many of you hung a stocking up as a child? This age-old custom originated in Holland. They celebrated St. Nicholas Day on December 6. St. Nicholas was a bishop in Asia who was very generous and shared what he had in secret. The children would sit their wooden shoes outside and the next morning they would awake to find them filled with fruit, nuts, and candy. Today we hang up our stockings on Christmas Eve, and the next morning they're filled with lots of goodies. (*Pause*) That is, if we've been good!

As the NARRATOR *speaks, a child brings in a large Christmas stocking. The child places it on the chancel rail and then takes a seat behind the chancel rail. Sing "Here Comes Santa Claus" (optional).*

NARRATOR: Many years ago, holly was used during the months of winter to bring cheer to winter's bleakness. Later, it came to symbolize the life of Christ. The red berries symbolize the blood he shed for our redemption, the prickly leaves for his crown of thorns. Today the holly is a favorite Christmas greenery.

As the NARRATOR *speaks, a child brings in holly. The child places it on the chancel rail and takes a seat behind the chancel rail. Sing "Deck the Halls."*

NARRATOR: Bells have been used for centuries in China to call people to worship. We hear a lot of bells during the Christmas season. (*If possible, have someone ring a big bell.*) Yes, there are big church bells, sleigh bells, (*Have the children ring jingle bells.*) and there are Salvation Army bell ringers on street corners ringing bells to help the needy.

Sing "Jingle Bells."

NARRATOR: Using candles is another old custom. Candles were lit in homes in Norway, Denmark, and Ireland. The burning flame in the dark reminded them of the coming of Christ Jesus, the Light of the World. Some believed that the candle would guide the Christ Child to their homes on Christmas Eve. Candles were also used in the Advent wreath. (*Point out the Advent wreath, if there is one.*)

As the NARRATOR *speaks, teens or adults light candles in the windows.*

NARRATOR: We've been told that St. Francis of Assisi arranged the very first nativity or manger scene in Italy. Because so many people could not read back then, St. Francis set up a manger scene in the village square. He used live animals to help tell the story of the birth of Jesus. Many, many people came to hear and see this Bible story in the thirteenth century.

As the NARRATOR *speaks, a child comes in carrying a wooden sheep. Another child comes in carrying the manger. Sing "Away in a Manger."*

NARRATOR: No matter what Christmas traditions we observe, the central fact remains: Christmas is the reason we celebrate Jesus' birthday. We can choose to keep Christ at the center of our traditions; we can make him welcome in our hearts and homes, as we remember that he is truly the reason for the season. Now let's listen to the old, old and true story of Jesus' birth as recorded in the Bible.

15

Someone reads Luke 2:1-7 as MARY *and* JOSEPH *enter slowly and sit in front of the manger. Sing "Silent Night."*

Someone reads Luke 2:8-9 as the SHEPHERDS *enter and gather to the left of the manger. An* ANGEL *appears.*

The ANGEL *reads Luke 2:10-12.*

Someone reads Luke 2:13. The choir reads in unison Luke 2:14.

Someone reads Luke 2:15-16 as the SHEPHERDS *go to the nativity scene and kneel. Sing "O Little Town of Bethlehem."*

Someone reads Luke 2:17-20 as the SHEPHERDS *leave.*

Someone reads Matthew 2:1-9 as the WISE MEN *enter slowly.*

Someone reads Matthew 2:10-12 as the WISE MEN *bring gifts to the manger scene and then leave. An* ANGEL *appears.*

READER: Now after they had left, an angel of the Lord appeared to Joseph in a dream and said . . .

ANGEL: Get up, take the child and his mother, and flee to Egypt, and remain there until I tell you: for Herod is about to search for the child, to destroy him.

Someone reads Matthew 2:14-15 and 2:23 as MARY *and* JOSEPH *leave. Sing "Go Tell It on the Mountain."*

NARRATOR: Thus, the old, old story of Jesus' birth that we have heard so many times. Now we want to invite everyone to stand and sing the first and last verses of "Joy to the World." Thank you for coming, and Merry Christmas.

The cast members gather up front during the hymn and take their bow.

The Midnight Miracle

By Shirley Lockhart Ingram

Production Notes

This drama requires only one setting: a town park with the nativity cast as a tableau. The nativity cast is frozen in one position until the midnight scene. Playing time is approximately thirty-five minutes.

Characters

Narrator	Mary
Grandmother	Joseph
Child 1 (elementary age)	Baby Jesus (could be a doll)
Child 2 (elementary age)	Wise Man 1
Skeptic (older child or adult)	Wise Man 2
Choir Leader	Wise Man 3
Carolers (singing only)	Shepherd 1
Teen 1	Shepherd 2
Teen 2	Shepherd 3

Extra shepherds (may be used to sit and listen)
Group of preschool and elementary-age children

Props

Manger, stool for Mary, Bible for the narrator, gifts for the wise men, spotlight, blankets, doll (or a real baby), four large boxes marked *PEACE, HOPE, JOY,* and *LOVE* (small pieces of paper or cards with these same words should be placed in the respective boxes.)

Costumes

Shoppers and carolers: regular modern-day clothes
Wise men: choir robes and crowns
Shepherds: bathrobes or sheets, sandals, staffs
Mary: bathrobes or sheets
Joseph: bathrobes or sheets

NARRATOR: It is the week before Christmas. Shoppers are rushing to and fro trying to get that last-minute

17

gift. The church chimes are playing traditional Christmas hymns. They are coming from the church that bought the nativity statues this year.

Lights are focused on the nativity cast. The NARRATOR *steps aside. A* GRANDMOTHER, *carrying a shopping bag, walks up to the scene and pauses.*

GRANDMOTHER: How lovely! I'm glad that the town church furnished the town with this scene. They look so real! Reminds me of when I was a young girl. (*Pulls her shawl tighter around her shoulder.*) We would act out the Christmas story at church. One year I got to play Mary. After the play, the church leaders would pass out a small brown sack of oranges, apples, and candy. I can still smell that orange. (*Sniffs*) I only wish my grandchildren could enjoy Christmas in the good old days like I did. Christmas has become too commercial.

GRANDMOTHER *walks off.* CHILD 1 *and* CHILD 2, *bundled up, walk by. They stop in front of the scene.*

CHILD 1: Look, there's baby Jesus.

CHILD 2: Yes, with Mary and Joseph.

CHILD 1: They look so real. Can't believe he was born in a manger.

CHILD 2: Yep, in Bethlehem. They couldn't find a hotel room.

CHILD 1: That must have been terrible!

CHILD 2: Jesus was born on Christmas Day. That's why we celebrate Christmas on that day.

CHILD 1: My Sunday school teacher says that if baby Jesus hadn't been born, we wouldn't have any Christmas.

CHILD 2: I'm sure glad he was, aren't you?

CHILD 1: Yes. We had better go. Our mothers will be worried about us.

CHILD 1 *and* CHILD 2 *walk offstage in the opposite direction of their entrance. A* SKEPTIC *ambles by, passing the scene. Looking back over his shoulder, he sees the scene, turns around, and comes back to it.*

SKEPTIC: Well, well, what have we here? Someone has added something to the town park this year. A man, woman, shepherds. (*Laughs*) Ha! Ha! Santa Claus on one corner (*Points*) and this crew on the other. Some preacher must have put this up. They keep trying to tell us that Jesus, a Jew, was sent by God to save the world (*Laughs*) No one can save this world! Bet he can't solve all my problems. They say that this happened over two thousand years ago. (*Shakes head doubtfully*) I just don't know. Don't know about all this.

SKEPTIC *exits in opposite direction of his entrance.* TEEN 1 *and* TEEN 2 *come strolling by with packages in hand. They stop and look at the scene.*

TEEN 1: Hey, look, John, a nativity scene. Gosh, they look real, don't they? Sorta spooky!

TEEN 2: Yeah, man! I heard that big church bought these statues. Say, don't you go to that church?

TEEN 1: Yes, I do. I'm proud of our church for doing this. Sorta' a reminder of the real meaning of Christmas, rather than all that Santa Claus and commercial stuff.

TEEN 2: Guess you're right. By the way, what are you getting for Christmas? I want a new CD player. My old one is torn up.

TEEN 1: Oh, I don't know. I don't really need anything. Our youth group is going to help a needy family this year, and I was going to help them, if I get any extra money to spend.

TEEN 2: You mean that you're going to give up part of your money to give to somebody you don't even know?

19

TEEN 1: Well, maybe not all of it, but a part of it. Isn't that what Christmas is all about? Giving?

TEEN 2: I don't know. Some people don't try to help themselves. Some are just too lazy to work. I still want that CD player.

TEEN 1: Say, why don't you join our youth group next Sunday evening and go caroling with us to the nursing home and some shut-ins? I always feel good after we do this. Come on and join us. Okay?

TEEN 2: Hey, man, I can't carry a tune in a bucket. I might come, though. Depends on what's going on. Better go. Almost supper time. Bye!

TEEN 1 and TEEN 2 exit in different directions. The CAROLERS enter from the back of the sanctuary, singing "Deck the Halls." When they reach the front pew, they stop and face the nativity scene. Then they turn around to face the congregation.

CHOIR LEADER: Now let's sing the carols we have been practicing here in front of the nativity scene.

CAROLERS sing "Away in a Manger," "It Came Upon the Midnight Clear," and "Silent Night." They kneel in front of the manger and then exit singing "Go Tell It on the Mountain." Other carols may be used.

The lights are dimmed. All is quiet. The organ or bells chime twelve times. Then the lights slowly get brighter. Suddenly the nativity characters begin to stretch and move.

SHEPHERD 1: Boy, I thought they would never leave. I'm tired. (*Yawns*)

SHEPHERD 2: I'm tired too. Cold sitting on this ground.

SHEPHERD 3: I'm tired and cold. (*Shivers*)

SHEPHERD 1: Here, Joseph, give this blanket to Mary.

SHEPHERD 1 hands a blanket to JOSEPH, who puts it around MARY's shoulder.

20

JOSEPH:	Thank you, sir.
MARY:	Thank you, Joseph. Would you get another wrap for the baby?

JOSEPH *gets another blanket and gives it to* MARY, *who lays it on* BABY JESUS. *The three* WISE MEN *enter, looking tired.*

WISE MAN 1:	Oh, finally, we found the Baby King!
SHEPHERD 1:	(*Looking skeptical*) And who are you?
WISE MAN 1:	We have come from the East searching for the young king. It has been a long journey.
WISE MAN 2:	We saw the big, bright star in the East and have followed it for many days and nights.
WISE MAN 3:	We have come to worship the new king and have brought him gifts.

Each WISE MAN *kneels in sequence and lays his gift in front of the manger.*

WISE MAN 1:	I bring him gold.
WISE MAN 2:	And I bring him frankincense. Ahh! (*Sniffs*)
WISE MAN 3:	Myrrh is my gift to him.

The WISE MEN *stand to one side.*

MARY:	Thank you very much.
JOSEPH:	Yes, thank you.
SHEPHERD 1:	Some people don't believe in this special baby.
SHEPHERD 2:	Their sense of giving and receiving gets confusing for the people.
SHEPHERD 3:	I wish the world could have been present tonight to feel the special spirit of this baby.

WISE MAN 1: Isaiah the prophet said that "a young woman shall conceive and bear a son and shall call his name Immanuel . . . For to us a child is born, to us a son is given; and the government shall be upon his shoulder, and his name will be called Wonderful Counselor, Mighty God, Everlasting Father, Prince of Peace."

WISE MAN 2: Do these twentieth century people not have ears to hear and eyes to see the handiwork and voice of God amidst them?

WISE MAN 3: I'm glad we don't live in this twentieth century . . . too much stress.

SHEPHERD 1: We don't have much, but we eat well, and we have a place to lay our head. These people constantly want something.

SHEPHERD 2: These people only think of getting more and more.

SHEPHERD 3: (*Looks at* WISE MAN 1) O wise man, if you were going to receive a gift, what would you want?

WISE MAN 1: (*Pauses and puts his hand under his chin*) I think if I had a choice, I would choose peace. Peace on earth. No more wars or conflict among humankind. (*Goes to one side of the stage and finds a box marked* PEACE *and places it on the chancel rail.*)

SHEPHERD 3: (*Nods toward* WISE MAN 2) What would you desire?

WISE MAN 2: We need peace. But I would like to receive the gift of hope. Hope from fear and hope for tomorrow. (*Goes to one side of the stage and finds a box marked* HOPE *and places it on the chancel rail.*)

SHEPHERD 3: (*Nods toward* WISE MAN 3) And you?

WISE MAN 3: We need peace and hope, but we also need joy. Joy to the world, the Lord is come. Joy should put a song in our hearts. Joy is the good news that God saves us.

(*Goes to one side of the stage and finds a box marked* JOY *and places it on the chancel rail.*)

SHEPHERD 3: (*Looks toward* SHEPHERDS 1 *and* 2) And brothers, what are we going to give and would like to receive?

SHEPHERDS 1 & 2: (*In unison*) Love!

SHEPHERD 3: Very good. I agree. The coming of the Christ Child is an invitation to love and to love others.

Again the nativity characters freeze in their positions. A bell chimes one time. TEENS 1 *and* 2 *come strolling back by.*

TEEN 1: Say, John, do you notice anything different about this scene?

TEEN 2: Hey, they've added the wise men! I remember they were the last to get to Bethlehem. Some of them have changed positions too.

TEEN 1: Boy, that's cool. How did they do that?

TEEN 2: What a variety of visitors Mary and Joseph had! The rich and the poor came to see Jesus. That includes all humankind!

TEEN 1: Right on, John.

TEENS 1 and 2 stand to one side.

NARRATOR: Peace, hope, joy, and love. What lovely gifts to receive and to give. We should treasure these gifts not just at Christmas time, but all year through. May you carry these gifts to your home tonight. Thank you.

Nativity characters and other players form a semi-circle while "Joy to the World" is being sung by the congregation. The WISE MEN *and* SHEPHERDS *take small cards with PEACE, HOPE, JOY, and LOVE out of the respective boxes and pass them out to the congregation in an orderly manner.*

Boys Can Be Angels Too

By Jo Carolyn Beebe; adapted by Diana Smith

Production Notes

This drama takes place in a church sanctuary or a social hall. The stool and the manger are stage center. The piano is left in view of the audience. Ladders or risers are near the piano, behind the Angel Choir. The Bible is on the lectern at stage right. Consider singing Christmas carols during intermission.

Characters

Speaking roles:
Brother Eugene Hankins
Billy Bob Galloway
Miss Annie Belle Stone
Sarah Kate Jessup
Violet Galloway
Mrs. Florine Waters
Wise Men

Nonspeaking roles:
Shepherds
Angel Choir
Mary
Joseph

Props

Manger; bale of hay or stool; two Bibles; lectern; piano, organ, or keyboard; ladder; three gifts for Wise Men; baby doll; fake campfire; two or three shepherd's staffs (optional: palm trees may be made from construction paper)

Costumes

Act One:
All actors: street clothes

Act Two:
Brother Eugene: ministerial vestment
Angel Choir: choir robe and garland halos
Sarah Kate: white angel outfit, wings, tiara
Shepherds: bathrobes (no floral or pastel)
Wise Men: bathrobes, crowns, necklaces, and so forth
Miss Annie Belle and Florine Waters: dress or suit. Both should have hats. Miss Annie Belle may have gloves.
Mary: robe and draped headwear
Joseph: robe and headpiece; carries staff, if available.

Act One

<u>Setting:</u> Rehearsal, prior to Christmas

MISS ANNIE BELLE *is in the audience, at the end of Row 2 or 3.*

BROTHER EUGENE *enters from stage right and goes to the lectern.* SHEPHERDS, *including* BILLY BOB GALLOWAY, *enter from stage right and crouch around an imaginary campfire.* MARY *and* JOSEPH *enter and move to stage center.* FLORINE WATERS *and the* ANGEL CHOIR *enter from stage left and gather near the piano.* FLORINE WATERS *is busy arranging* ANGEL CHOIR *members into their places with a certain amount of confusion.* SARAH JANE *is several steps up on the ladder. Three* WISE MEN *enter from the back of the hall or the sanctuary. They can be seated in the last row.*

The ANNOUNCER *enters from stage left and goes stage front and center.*

ANNOUNCER: We are pleased to present the annual Christmas pageant, which is called "Boys Can Be Angels." This is a play in two acts. Act One takes place during rehearsal for the play. Act Two is the final production. There will be a short intermission, during which we ask that you remain seated.

The ANNOUNCER *exits stage left.*

BROTHER EUGENE: ". . . Some shepherds were in the fields outside the village, guarding their flocks of sheep. Suddenly an angel appeared among them, and the landscape shone bright with the glory of the Lord. They were badly frightened, but the angel reassured them. 'Don't be afraid!' he said. 'I bring you the most joyful news ever . . .'"

BILLY BOB: Excuse me! Excuse me!

MISS ANNIE BELLE *stands from the congregation.*

MISS ANNIE BELLE: Who said that? What young gentleman had the discourtesy to interrupt the reading of the Scripture?

MISS ANNIE BELLE *walks to the front of the church/hall.* BILLY BOB *stands.*

25

BILLY BOB: I did, Miss Annie Belle. Did I hear right? Did Brother Eugene say that angel was a HE?

MISS ANNIE BELLE: Billy Bob Galloway, what *are* you talking about?

BILLY BOB: Well, Brother Eugene was reading about that angel who appeared before the shepherds, and he said the angel was a "he." At least, that's what I thought he said.

MISS ANNIE BELLE *turns to* BROTHER EUGENE *at the lectern.*

MISS ANNIE BELLE: Brother Eugene, pardon the interruption. I know your time is valuable, and we do so appreciate your help in our little Christmas presentation.

BROTHER EUGENE: Miss Annie Belle, this is what rehearsals are for, and we always hope that the children are learning as they perform the Bible stories. Now, let's see if we can straighten this out. (*Steps from behind the lectern and walks to* BILLY BOB) Now what is your problem, young man? Billy Bob, do you have a question about the narration?

BILLY BOB: (*Looks uncomfortable*) Well, yes, sir. Did you say the angel was a man?

BROTHER EUGENE: (*Points to the Bible in his hand*) That's what this version of the Bible says.

BILLY BOB: Well, how come Sarah Kate Jessup is standing over there being the head angel? She's always the head angel, and if the Bible says the angel is a "he," then it ought to be a boy over there. The Bible says so.

SARAH KATE *looks upset.*

BROTHER EUGENE: Now, Billy Bob, Miss Annie Belle is an expert on the theater. Why, she took a course in theater appreciation at _____ (*Fills in the name of a local college*). I'm sure she knows what's best.

26

MISS ANNIE BELLE: (*Looks exasperated*) Billy Bob Galloway, Christmas is almost here, and we all have a lot to do, like baking and shopping. Now, you and your sister, Violet, are just visiting your grandparents and don't regularly go to our church. So you shouldn't be interfering in this pageant. Do you *really* want to be an angel?

BILLY BOB: (*Excitedly*) Well, heck, yeah, Miss Annie Belle. Boys can be angels. It says so in the Bible. A boy should be the head angel.

BROTHER EUGENE *chuckles.* SARAH KATE *is upset.* MISS ANNIE BELLE *is stunned.*

SARAH KATE: (*Whining*) But I'm always the head angel. Girls are always angels, and boys are always shepherds. Miss Annie Belle, you're not going to let him be an angel, are you?

MISS ANNIE BELLE: Oh, he doesn't really want to be an angel — do you, Billy Bob?

BILLY BOB: Why not?

BROTHER EUGENE *checks his watch, clears his throat, and snaps his fingers.*

BROTHER EUGENE: Oh, gee! I'm sorry, Miss Annie Belle, but I have to go. I'm past due meeting my wife at _____ (*Fills in the name of a local store*) to shop for our needy families. I'm sure you'll clear this up by the time I return. Bye, Miss Annie Belle. Bye, children.

BROTHER EUGENE *hurries out the door.*

The ANGEL CHOIR *members on stage are getting restless. One lies down. Others play hand games. Some giggle and whisper.*

SARAH KATE: (*Wails*) But *I'm* supposed to be the angel.

MISS ANNIE BELLE *stands in front of* BILLY BOB, *hands on her hips.*

MISS ANNIE BELLE: Now, Billy Bob, of course there are men angels mentioned in the Bible. There was Michael, and there was Gabriel, but *we* always have girls be angels in *our* Christmas plays.

BILLY BOB: Yes, ma'am, I know that, but it'll look funny for Brother Eugene to read "he said" and have Sarah Kate as the angel.

SARAH KATE: Why, people won't even pay attention to what Brother Eugene is reading when they see that my Mama bought me new wings and borrowed Jane Marie Smythe's rhinestone tiara that she wore in the Miss _____ (*Fills in the name of your state*) pageant.

MISS ANNIE BELLE: Of course, Sarah Kate. She's right, Billy Bob. Your mother won't have time to make you an angel costume, and you can just wear your bathrobe to be a shepherd.

BILLY BOB: Well, I'm thinking that I owe it to the men of the world to be the head angel in this play, so . . .

MISS ANNIE BELLE: Oh, for goodness sakes! (*Stamps foot. Turns to* FLORINE WATERS *at the keyboard*) Florine, please practice with the girls. Shepherds, go to the restroom. Quietly!

The SHEPHERDS *exit — all except* BILLY BOB, *who sneaks to the back row of the* ANGEL CHOIR. *From the back of the sanctuary/hall, the three* WISE MEN *call out.*

WISE MAN 1: Miss Annie Belle! Miss Annie Belle!

WISE MAN 2: What about us?

WISE MAN 3: Yeah! What about us?

MISS ANNIE BELLE: Oh, I'm sorry, children. Wait, wait, Mrs. Waters. Joseph and the wise men, go to the restroom with the shepherds. Mary, you sing with the angels.

JOSEPH *and the* WISE MEN *exit with the* SHEPHERDS. FLORINE WATERS *is trying to organize the girls.* MARY *comes to join them.* BILLY BOB*'s sister,* VIOLET, *pulls* BILLY BOB *to the side.*

VIOLET: Billy Bob, you are in *soooo* much trouble. I'm going to tell Mama that you messed up the Christmas play.

BILLY BOB: I didn't mess up the play. I'm just making it the way it's supposed to be like in the Bible.

VIOLET: Oh, you think you know everything — like the time you cleaned Papa's car with the Brillo pads, and he thought he scraped the bushes. I'm going to tell.

MISS ANNIE BELLE: Violet! You go back with the angels. Billy Bob, you're with the shepherds. (*Quickly exits stage right. The* ANGEL CHOIR, MARY, *and* BILLY BOB *gather around* FLORINE WATERS *and sing a Christmas carol.* MISS ANNIE BELLE *enters with a different Bible in her hands. She looks pleased. She holds up the Bible.*)

MISS ANNIE BELLE: Yes, we'll use this version — Luke, chapter 2, verse 10: "And the angel said to them . . ."

FLORINE WATERS: (*Excitedly*) I wish you'd listen to this child sing. (*Puts her arm on Billy Bob's shoulders*) Why, he sings like . . .

MISS ANNIE BELLE: Don't tell me. He sings like an angel?

FLORINE WATERS: Why, he surely does. I just about died from surprise. We just have to have him sing a solo.

MISS ANNIE BELLE: Billy Bob, do you like to sing?

BILLY BOB: Yes, ma'am. I sing in the glee club at my school. Does this mean that I get to be head angel?

VIOLET: Billy Bob, I'm going to tell. I am, as sure as Christmas is coming.

MISS ANNIE BELLE *sits down with her head in her hands. Then she rises.*

MISS ANNIE BELLE: Rehearsal is over for the day. You go on home now.

FLORINE WATERS: Come on, angels. Let's go.

End of scene. All exit.

Intermission

Act Two

FLORINE WATERS *and the* ANGEL CHOIR *enter stage left and take their places.* BILLY BOB *enters with the* ANGEL CHOIR, *but stands toward the back, so the audience is not aware.* SARAH KATE *takes her place on the ladder.* BROTHER EUGENE *goes to the lectern carrying* MISS ANNIE BELLE*'s Bible.* MISS ANNIE BELLE *stands to one side of stage with a clipboard. All freeze.*

ANNOUNCER: We now join the Christmas pageant in progress.

BROTHER EUGENE: "God sent the angel Gabriel to Nazareth, a town in Galilee, to a virgin pledged to be married to a man named Joseph, a descendant of David. The virgin's name was Mary. In those days Caesar Augustus issued a decree that a census should be taken of the entire Roman world. And everyone went to his own town to register."

JOSEPH *and* MARY, *carrying a baby, start to walk slowly from the back of the sanctuary/hall to stage center. They take their places as* BROTHER EUGENE *continues to read.*

BROTHER EUGENE: "So Joseph also went up from the town of Nazareth in Galilee to Judea, to Bethlehem the town of David, because he belonged to the house and line of David. He went there to register with Mary, who was pledged to be married to him and was expecting a child. While they were there, the time came for the baby to be born, and she gave birth to her firstborn, a son. She wrapped him in clothes and placed him in a manger, because there was no room for them in the inn."

The SHEPHERDS *enter and crouch down around the campfire, stage right.* SARAH KATE *moves toward the* SHEPHERDS *and raises her arms.*

BROTHER EUGENE: "And there were shepherds living out in the fields nearby, keeping watch over their flocks at night. An angel of the Lord appeared to them, and the glory of the Lord shone around them, and they were terrified. But the angel said to them, 'Do not be afraid. I bring you good news of great joy that will be for all the people. Today in the town of David a Savior has been born to you; he is Christ the Lord. This will be a sign to you: You will find a baby wrapped in cloths and lying in a manger.' Suddenly a great company of the heavenly host appeared with the angel, praising God and saying, 'Glory to God in the highest, and on earth peace to men on whom his favor rests.'"

SARAH KATE joins the ANGEL CHOIR. *The* ANGEL CHOIR *sings an appropriate carol.*

BROTHER EUGENE: "When the angels had left them and gone into heaven, the shepherds said to one another, 'Let's go to Bethlehem and see this thing that has happened, which the Lord has told us about.' So they hurried off and found Mary and Joseph and the baby, who was lying in the manger."

The SHEPHERDS *move to the manger. The* WISE MEN *enter and pause, away from the manger.*

BROTHER EUGENE: "Magi from the east came to Jerusalem and asked, 'Where is the one who has been born king of the Jews? We saw his star in the east and have come to worship him.' . . . And the star they had seen . . . went ahead of them until it stopped over the place where the child was. When they saw the star they were overjoyed."

The WISE MEN *continue to the manger.*

BROTHER EUGENE: "On coming to the house, they saw the child with his mother Mary, and they bowed down and worshiped him. Then they opened their treasure and presented him with gifts of gold and of incense and myrrh."

The WISE MEN *present gifts. The* ANGELS, SHEPHERDS, WISE MEN, MARY, *and* JOSEPH *all sing (suggestion: "Adestes Fidelis").* BILLY BOB *sings the second verse alone. At the conclusion of the carol,* MISS ANNIE BELLE, *standing at one side of the stage, turns to the audience and speaks.*

MISS ANNIE BELLE: Boys *can* be angels.

BROTHER EUGENE: Miss Annie Belle, you are so right. Now, will everyone rise and sing?

Sing "Joy to the World" or another appropriate carol. The cast may exit during the carol.